Pirelli Calendar Classics

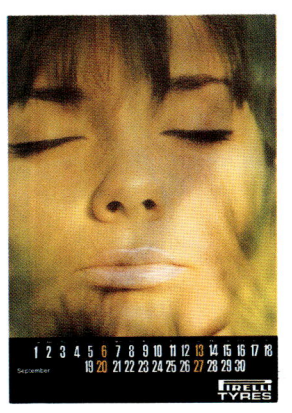

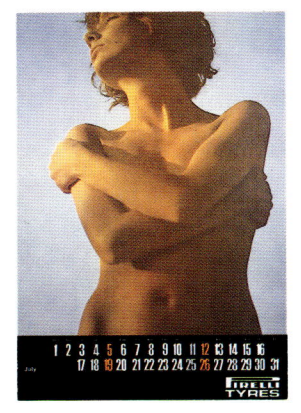

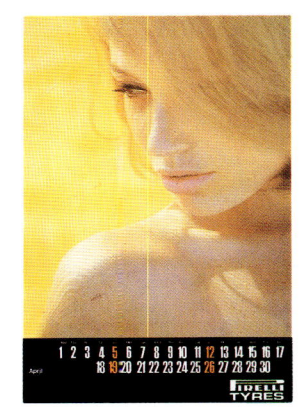

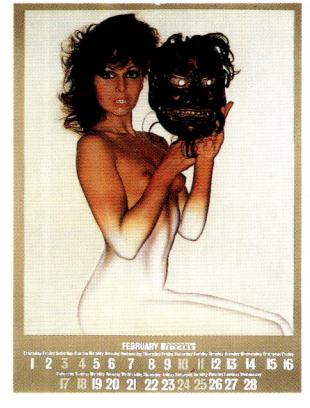

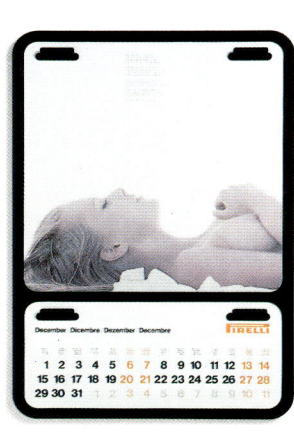

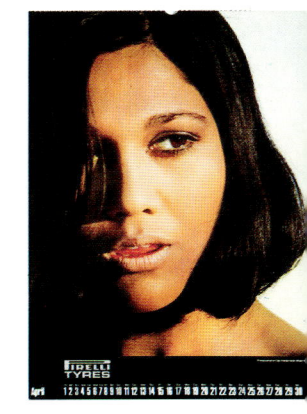
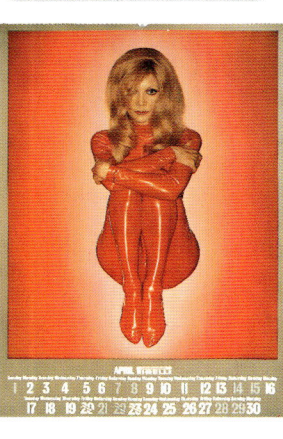

Pirelli Calendar Classics

100 PHOTOGRAPHS FROM THE FIRST 30 YEARS

BCA

LONDON   NEW YORK   SYDNEY   TORONTO

*Grateful thanks are due to Gioacchino del Balzo of Pirelli for his support in seeing
this through, and to Robert Newman, also of Pirelli, for his original idea...*
Derek Forsyth

This edition published 1993 by BCA by arrangement with
PAVILION BOOKS LIMITED

CN 5625

First published in Great Britain in 1993 by
PAVILION BOOKS LIMITED

Caption quotations from *The Pirelli Calendar Album*
(Text Copyright © Michael Pye 1988) by kind permission of Curtis Brown,
London, on behalf of the author.

designers
Erica Hare
Seymour Quilter

editorial consultant
Andrew Best

Colour separation by CLG, Italy

Printed and bound in Italy by New Interlitho

PREFACE

I still find it hard to believe that I invented a calendar that would stretch the imagination and at the same time become a marketing phenomenon. All the way I have been supported by Pirelli's extraordinary faith in what I might do. That has been a luxury indeed and I am grateful for it. I want also to say that these calendars could not have happened without the patient skills of those who took the photographs, and of those who contributed to the increasingly complex shoots — such as make-up artists and stylists, and always the models. I then took a back seat and watched the calendar become year by year a creature of increasing artifice. I wonder at it still, and I still wonder that Pirelli wants me to try my hand for 1994. I remain grateful, not least for the opportunity to bring together and design this book.

DEREK FORSYTH 1993

INTRODUCTION

By Gioacchino del Balzo

The opportunity to introduce this collection of classic photographs from thirty years of the Pirelli Calendar affords me great pleasure. The more so because the Pirelli Calendar has always enjoyed a reputation far wider than the select circle of those individuals and companies who have received it over the years. Pirelli Calendars cannot be begged, nor can they be bought – except secondhand and then at high prices.

So what is it that makes the Pirelli Calendar so special? I believe that since its inception under the direction of Derek Forsyth the Pirelli Calendar has reflected and continues to reflect the spirit of the age. I might even suggest that it has often anticipated it. The Pirelli Calendar first went abroad, when abroad was for most unreachable, and it brought back friendly snapshots from the beach. When the package tour became popular, Pirelli went further afield to Tunisia, California and the Caribbean, growing ever more sophisticated in its reflection of the lifestyles and graphic trends of the times. Then came a reaction away from sexuality with Sarah Moon's 1972 shoot. With its ambiguous hint of narrative and impressionist, romantic tone, her calendar marked an astonishing change of stance. The next calendar was astonishing in a different way: Allen Jones' compilation was called 'camp, perverse, brilliant'. Derek Forsyth's last calendar and, it seemed at the time, Pirelli's was Hans Feurer's warm and intimate Seychelles shoot in 1974.

When the calendar came back ten years later, Pirelli had moved the goalposts: the calendar must focus on the Pirelli tyre. Art director Martyn Walsh accomplished this in an almost subliminal way, each year reflecting the tread of the tyre in the new generation of calendars. Increasingly he brought the calendars into the studio and imposed coherent, consistent themes. Once again, the calendars proved a sounding-board for the times; women's independence, their heroism and, with the upcoming Barcelona Olympic Games in mind, their athletic skills. The ballet contrived by Gillian Lynne for the 1988 calendar was brilliantly captured in Barry Lategan's photographs.

What next? For 1994 Pirelli has decided to pay tribute to the woman of today. It has also decided to entrust Derek Forsyth with its next calendar. Watch this space...

GIOACCHINO DEL BALZO
Marketing Manager
PIRELLI LIMITED

1964

photographer
ROBERT FREEMAN

location
MAJORCA

month
MARCH

For this first Pirelli Calendar, the new naturalness was everything – in
reaction to the spiky artifice of 1950s studio shots. But it was by no
means naïve… The detail still had to be recognisably,
enticingly, a woman.

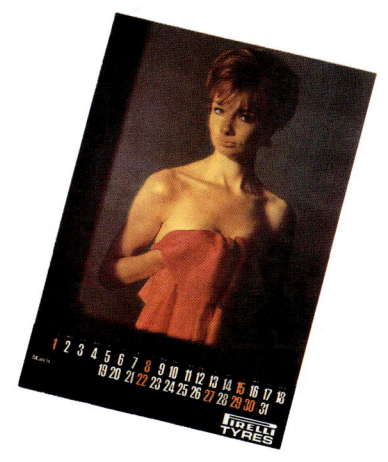

1964

photographer
ROBERT FREEMAN

location
MAJORCA

month
APRIL

'There was no really big deal about it,' says model Jane Lumb, a student at the time. 'We were off to Majorca for a week to make some nice pictures. But I did think that if every job was going to be like this, modelling would suit me very well.'

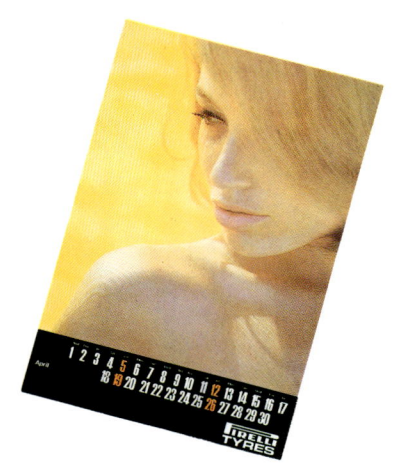

1 9 6 4

photographer
ROBERT FREEMAN

location
MAJORCA

month
JULY

'If you like girls, then they're flowers in the garden – there are different
moods and moments, and it's nice to capture them.'
(Robert Freeman)

1964

photographer
ROBERT FREEMAN

location
MAJORCA

month
AUGUST

Robert Freeman had been a professional for only two years. Soon he
was to fix that early image of the Beatles on their first album covers.

1964

photographer
ROBERT FREEMAN

location
MAJORCA

month
SEPTEMBER

'There could be things going on either in her mind or outside
the frame.'
(Robert Freeman)

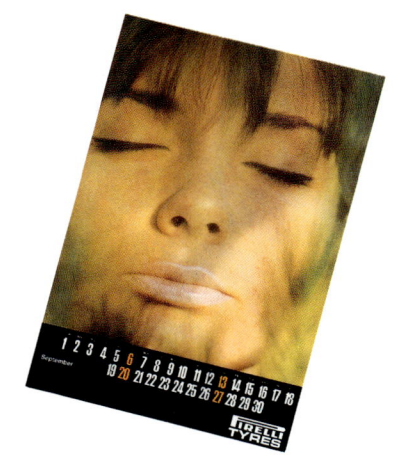

1964

photographer
ROBERT FREEMAN

location
MAJORCA

month
DECEMBER

'We thought of a graphic approach, close-ups, parts of bodies,
simple and intimate.'
(Robert Freeman)

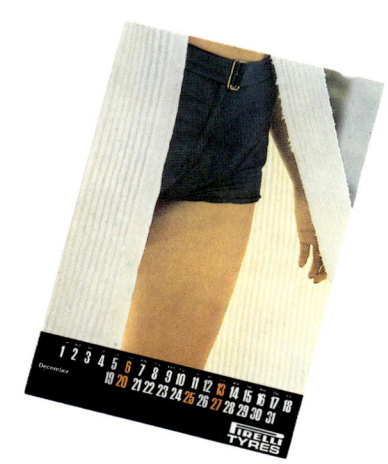

1965

photographer
BRIAN DUFFY

location
SOUTH OF FRANCE

month
MARCH

'The way to do a calendar with a fairly high element of sex was to put
the girls in some natural setting like the beach.'
(Colin Forbes, designer)

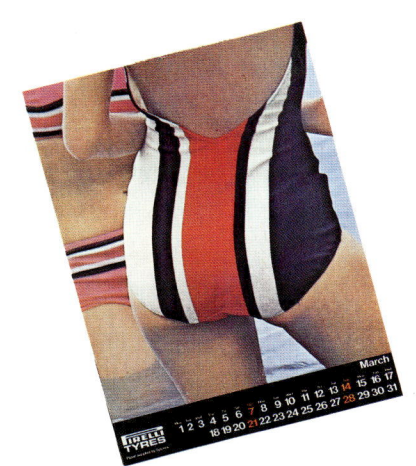

1965

photographer
BRIAN DUFFY

location
SOUTH OF FRANCE

month
JUNE

Along with David Bailey and Terence Donovan, Brian Duffy was one of
three star photographers from London's East End.

1965

photographer
BRIAN DUFFY

location
SOUTH OF FRANCE

month
OCTOBER

Brian Duffy drove a Sprite, in which he gave model Pauline Stone a lift
to Monaco. 'It helps that Duffy made women look beautiful. He was
actually nice to women.'
(Pauline Stone)

1965

photographer
BRIAN DUFFY

location
SOUTH OF FRANCE

month
NOVEMBER

'We work from flair…,' said Brian Duffy at the time. But his eye and timing were very precise. The girl in a café, lighting a cigarette, could be called a cliché of French life. The tension is the picture.

1965

photographer
BRIAN DUFFY

location
SOUTH OF FRANCE

month
DECEMBER

At the window of the Monaco apartment where the Calendar team
stayed. This picture caused a sensation at the time.

1966

photographer
PETER KNAPP

location
MOROCCO

month
MARCH

'You have to remember that in the Sixties it was the beginning
of taking a plane and going to another town...
All of a sudden you could do it each week.'
(Peter Knapp)

1 9 6 6

photographer
PETER KNAPP

location
MOROCCO

month
APRIL

'I'm not so keen on making sex pictures. I often think people
are very interested by the girl.'
(Peter Knapp)

1966

photographer
PETER KNAPP

location
MOROCCO

month
MAY

At *Elle* Knapp had abandoned the chic, affected poses of the Fifties;
he made pictures that were more realistic and more sensual.

1 9 6 8

photographer
HARRI PECCINOTTI

location
TUNISIA

month
FEBRUARY

This morning I will not
Comb my hair.
It has lain
Pillowed on the hand of my lover.
(Kakinomoto No Hitomaro, eighth century)

Each picture in this Calendar was accompanied by a poem.

This morning I will not
Comb my hair.
It has lain
Pillowed on the hand of my lover.

KAKINOMOTO NO HITOMARO 697–707

1 9 6 8

photographer
HARRI PECCINOTTI

location
TUNISIA

month
AUGUST

You are the bouquet of your own bouquet:
The fairest flower that's there mid grace and green
Since from your breath the fragrance caught its sheen;
For it, like me, is pale with love all day.
(Pierre Ronsard, 1524-1585)

You are the bouquet of your own bouquet;
The fairest flower that's there mid grace and green
Since from your breath the fragrance caught its sheen;
For it, like me, is pale with love all day.

If then a flower may love you too, I say
(And all inept your virtue how to glean)
How should I feel who all your charms have seen,
Who grieve and serve in knowledge as I may?

E'en as a flower is withered in a day,
I fear your love will wither all too soon:
A woman's love is fickle as the moon.

Whatever destiny shall bring my way,
He cannot steal my memory of you—
Unless he tear my mind and heart out too.

PIERRE DE RONSARD 1524–1585

1968

photographer
HARRI PECCINOTTI

location
TUNISIA

month
OCTOBER

Whenas in silks my Julia goes,
Then, then (me thinks) how sweetly flowes
That liquefaction of her clothes.
(Robert Herrick, 1591-1674)

A voluminous, dark figure, double-exposed. In the background
a traditional Mahgreb house.

When as in silks my Julia goes,
Then, then (me thinks) how sweetly flowes
That liquefaction of her clothes.

Next, when I cast mine eyes and see
That brave Vibration each way free;
O how that glittering taketh me!

ROBERT HERRICK 1591–1674

Designed for Pirelli by Omnific

1968

photographer
HARRI PECCINOTTI

location
TUNISIA

month
DECEMBER

Yestreen as you lay down you vowed to be
Up and awake ere I might stir today;
But dawn's own dreams which fair maids ever see
Hold your eyes shut and wakefulness away.
See, see, a hundred times I kiss your eyes,
Your little breast: My love, 'tis morn! Arise!
(Pierre Ronsard, 1524-1585)

Come, up! and see the grassy dewiness,
Your rose tree all with budding blossoms hung,
The darling pinks you watered one by one
With your own hand last night in gentleness!

Yestreen as you lay down you vowed to be
Up and awake ere I might stir to day;
But dawn's own dreams which fair maids ever see

Hold your eyes shut and wakefulness away.
See, see, a hundred times I kiss your eyes,
Your little breast: My love, 'tis morn! Arise!

PIERRE DE RONSARD 1524–1585

1969

photographer
HARRI PECCINOTTI

location
CALIFORNIA

month
JANUARY

'Everywhere you turned on the beach there were incredible looking
girls doing whatever they felt like – it was a very free time. I said we
wouldn't have to take models or anything; we'd just go and photograph
people having a good time in the sun.'
(Harri Peccinotti)

1969

photographer
HARRI PECCINOTTI

location
CALIFORNIA

month
MARCH

There were no model agencies in Los Angeles, and the would-be starlets
were unused to the idea of still pictures that didn't lead to
moving pictures.

1969

photographer
HARRI PECCINOTTI

location
CALIFORNIA

month
MAY

Most of the Calendar was snatched on freeways, on the pier at Muscle
Beach, at Newport by Peccinotti's own favourite jazz clubs.

Pirelli Limited Pirelli House 343 Euston Road London NW1
Design, Art Direction and Production by Omnific Limited, England

1969

photographer
HARRI PECCINOTTI

location
CALIFORNIA

month
JULY

'We thought of doing the whole Calendar around the mouth,' said
Derek Forsyth. But no corporate board could have approved it.

1970

photographer
FRANCIS GIACOBETTI

location
BAHAMAS

month
JANUARY

Giacobetti had helped to found *Lui* and was consultant to *Playboy*.
'On *Lui* we were three friends working together,' he says. 'We took
girls all over the world and we made fantasies.'

1970

photographer
FRANCIS GIACOBETTI

location
BAHAMAS

month
FEBRUARY

'We knew the real reason for the Calendar was the garage,' says
Giacobetti. Derek Forsyth was art directing and creating the Calendar
alone for the first time, and he wanted something dramatic with a
strong reek of sexuality.

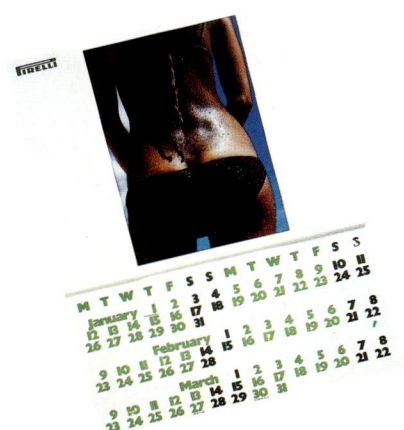

1970

photographer
FRANCIS GIACOBETTI

location
BAHAMAS

month
APRIL

'I am a voyeur. The pleasure is to look.'
(Giacobetti)

1970

photographer
FRANCIS GIACOBETTI

location
BAHAMAS

month
MAY

This Calendar was the first to be fully directed, like a film.
The boundary between still and movie technology – and thinking –
was breaking down.

1970

photographer
FRANCIS GIACOBETTI

location
BAHAMAS

month
JUNE

Derek Forsyth had encouraged Giacobetti to stretch technique.
The Calendar had come of age, and was to win the approval of the
public as well as of the trade.

1970

photographer
FRANCIS GIACOBETTI

location
BAHAMAS

month
JULY

A stunning example of Giacobetti's use of the new wide-angle lens and of the special filters that he devised to capture the drama of sea and sky.

1970

photographer
FRANCIS GIACOBETTI

location
BAHAMAS

month
AUGUST

Alexandra Bastedo, one of the models on the shoot, did not approve.
'The poses were tame by today's standards, but I thought they were
suggestive.' Here the model is Paula Martine.

1970

photographer
FRANCIS GIACOBETTI

location
BAHAMAS

month
SEPTEMBER

'We just did graphic things on a beach. Derek and I were
graphics snobs.'
(Giacobetti)

1970

photographer
FRANCIS GIACOBETTI

location
BAHAMAS

month
OCTOBER

It was still very unusual to feature black models, and this choice of
picture was a deliberate gesture that would be realised to the full
in Donovan's 1987 Calendar.

1970

photographer
FRANCIS GIACOBETTI

location
BAHAMAS

month
NOVEMBER

The graphic sense shared by art director and photographer took such
pictures far away from the simple and natural.

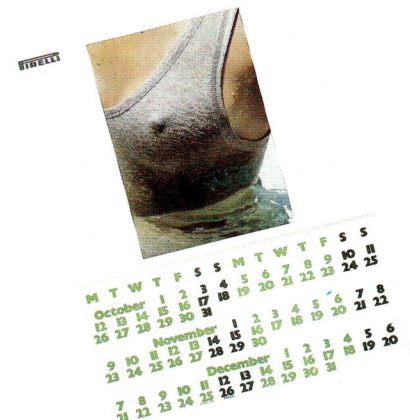

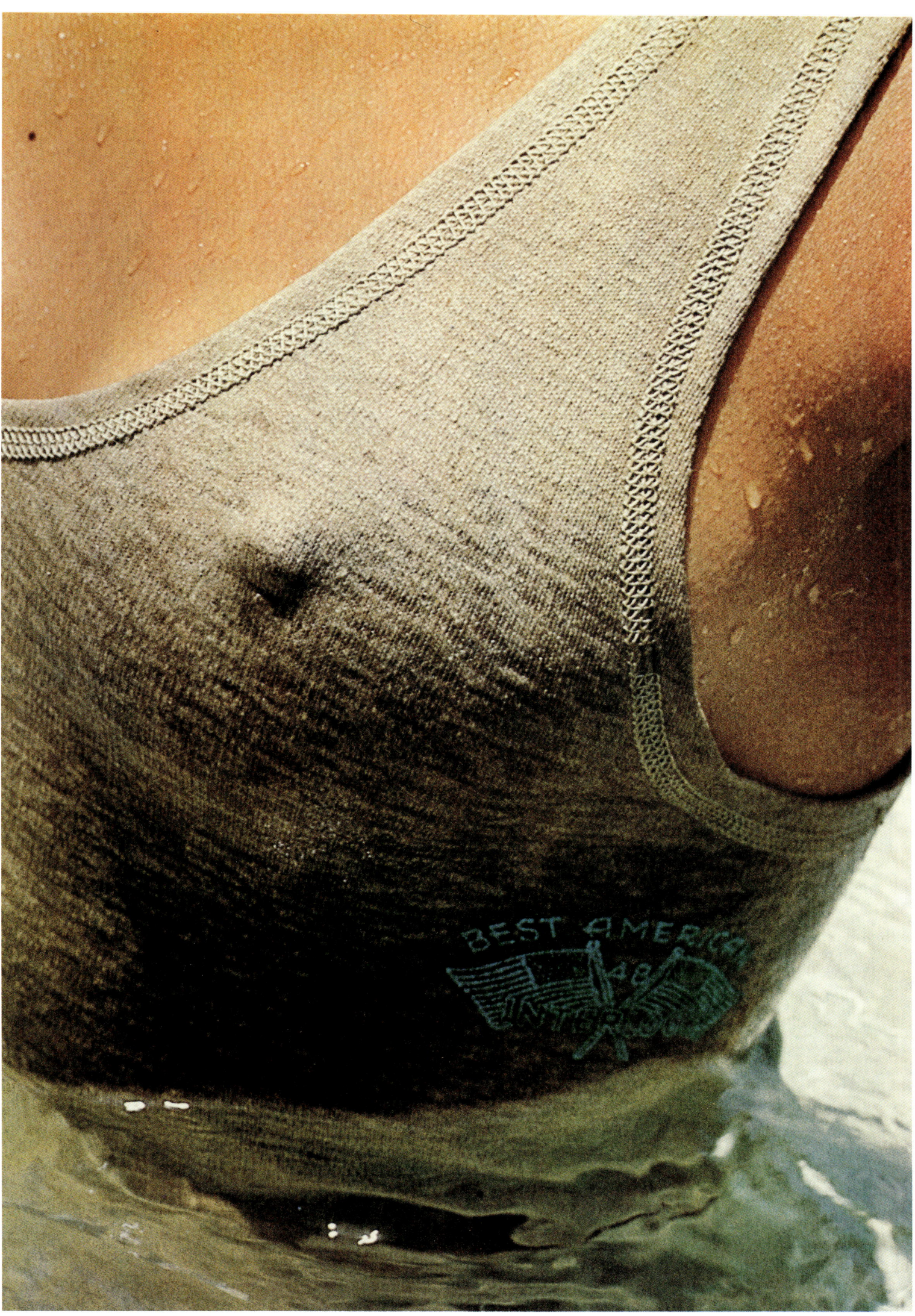

1970

photographer
FRANCIS GIACOBETTI

location
BAHAMAS

month
DECEMBER

Giacobetti knew the perfect crystalline seas around the Bahamas from
fashion pictures he had made for *Nova*.

1971

photographer
FRANCIS GIACOBETTI

location
JAMAICA

month
JANUARY

The models stayed in a grand, stone plantation house with its own
private beach. 'The girls were alone,' Giacobetti remembers.
'They were lost and the atmosphere was very strange.'

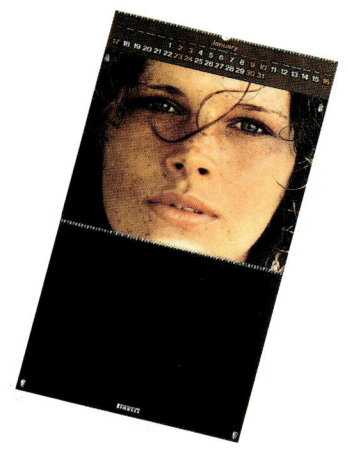

1971

photographer
FRANCIS GIACOBETTI

location
JAMAICA

month
APRIL

At night, Kate Howard kept her door shut so as not to see who might
be creeping where.

1971

photographer
FRANCIS GIACOBETTI

location
JAMAICA

month
APRIL

The girls wore long, almost Victorian lace gowns that happened to be
a little transparent.

1 9 7 1

photographer
FRANCIS GIACOBETTI

location
JAMAICA

month
JUNE

In contrast to the white sand of the Bahamas, the black volcanic sand
of this beach is unique to Jamaica, and echoes the dark, sultry
atmosphere of the shoot.

1971

photographer
FRANCIS GIACOBETTI

location
JAMAICA

month
AUGUST

'I do not have a sweet feeling about that place. It was very beautiful
until nightfall, but it was *angoissant*, disturbing.'
(Giacobetti)

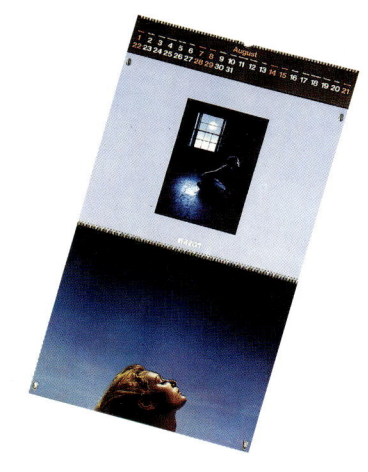

1971

photographer
FRANCIS GIACOBETTI

location
JAMAICA

month
OCTOBER

At night it was almost too hot to sleep, and the house stayed
edgily awake...

1971

photographer
FRANCIS GIACOBETTI

location
JAMAICA

month
DECEMBER

The Calendar was launched to an eager press, with rum punch and girls
in plantation dresses. Pirelli sometimes wondered whether it was worth
actually printing the Calendar when so many column inches came
from this one event.

1972

photographer
SARAH MOON

location
PARIS

month
JANUARY

By now the first Page Three girls were in the *Sun* and men's magazines
displayed women as if they were anatomical specimens. Derek Forsyth
had to ask himself: What next? Sarah Moon's Calendar marks a
total change of stance and direction, a return to the
'fragile, ornate woman of the past'.

1972

photographer
SARAH MOON

location
PARIS

month
APRIL

Derek Forsyth chose to work in a derelict house in a Paris suburb,
which had lain empty since the liberation. Sarah Moon found
the props and the decor in the flea markets.

1972

photographer
SARAH MOON

location
PARIS

month
MAY

'Seduction is the limit, and it is what you must achieve. You have a very
short time to succeed or miss, and you can't miss.'
(Sarah Moon)

1972

photographer
SARAH MOON

location
PARIS

month
AUGUST

The brief for the Calendar was to create an atmosphere of mystery set
in the not too distant past. 'It was summer and it was like being in
a no man's land,' remembers Sarah Moon. Almost nothing in her
work is accidental.

1972

photographer
SARAH MOON

location
PARIS

month
DECEMBER

This Calendar was later to be criticised by Pirelli as
'too romantic and unsexy.'

1973

artist
ALLEN JONES WITH PHILIP CASTLE

location
LONDON

month
JANUARY

For this Calendar Derek Forsyth forged a remarkable alliance between Brian Duffy, photographer, the artist Allen Jones, then notorious for some sculptures that turned women into hatstands or the crouching support of a table, and the airbrush artist Philip Castle, whose role was to bring Jones's sketches and Duffy's photographs together in a series of multimedia images.

1973

artist
ALLEN JONES WITH PHILIP CASTLE

location
LONDON

month
FEBRUARY

In the early Sixties the pin-up had already presented Allen Jones with a new possibility for representing the female figure in art. This Calendar pays conscious homage to Vargas, the master of the airbrush pin-up featured in *Esquire* magazine.

1 9 7 3

artist
ALLEN JONES WITH PHILIP CASTLE

location
LONDON

month
APRIL

Allen Jones was intrigued by the possibility of manipulating processes
available to him in his normal studio practice to produce a unique
product that could exist only as the Calendar.

1973

artist
ALLEN JONES WITH PHILIP CASTLE

location
LONDON

month
MAY

'The intention was that the Calendar would not look out of place on
the garage wall, and that, after a month of tea breaks, an interested
mechanic might reflect on the mechanics of seeing.'
(Derek Forsyth)

1973

artist

ALLEN JONES WITH PHILIP CASTLE

location

LONDON

month

JUNE

Philip Castle had discovered the airbrush at art school from the
fabulous sheen on car advertisements in 1950s magazines.

1973

artist
ALLEN JONES WITH PHILIP CASTLE

location
LONDON

month
JULY

Philip Castle had already made a famous poster of Elvis Presley and
produced the sinister posters for the movie *A Clockwork Orange*.

1973

artist
ALLEN JONES WITH PHILIP CASTLE

location
LONDON

month
AUGUST

Surprised, but not by joy. Philip Castle has supplanted the model's
head with a mask of alarm, as if to animate the girl on the
pinball machine.

1973

artist
ALLEN JONES WITH PHILIP CASTLE

location
LONDON

month
SEPTEMBER

Model Jane Lumb feels uneasy now about the way she's made to seem
blatantly available. But Allen Jones saw the Calendar as a chance to
turn the conventions of the pin-up into a pictorial lesson.

1 9 7 3

artist
ALLEN JONES WITH PHILIP CASTLE

location
LONDON

month
OCTOBER

A striking example of Philip Castle's airbrush skill. She wears a tiger-stripe swimsuit. The swimsuit dissolves away… Or is it creeping upwards to envelop her?

1973

artist
ALLEN JONES WITH PHILIP CASTLE

location
LONDON

month
NOVEMBER

'Allen Jones and Derek Forsyth virtually stood by me as I was working,'
Castle says. He took enlarged prints, and traced Jones's sketches over
Duffy's photographs – a marriage which required great tact.

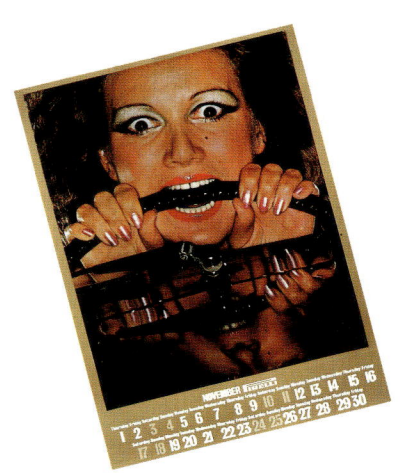

1973

artist
ALLEN JONES AND PHILIP CASTLE

location
LONDON

month
DECEMBER

The launch at the Marlborough Gallery was a riot of controversy.
People fought to get free calendars and champagne.

1974

photographer
HANS FEURER

location
SEYCHELLES

month
FEBRUARY

Pirelli's sales department now wanted pictures 'both human and
realistic'. A company report had criticised the previous Calendar
as 'erotic and objectionable'.

1974

photographer
HANS FEURER

location
SEYCHELLES

month
MARCH

Feurer's pictures feel truly free, and not just licensed to expose more
detail of the body. 'Feurer took away the keyhole aspect.'
(Barry Lategan)

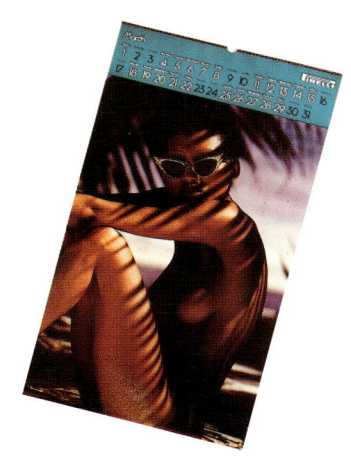

1974

photographer
HANS FEURER

location
SEYCHELLES

month
APRIL

Hans Feurer's pictures are immensely likeable. He himself explains:
'I like women'. He likes them so well that his images transcend any
thought of posed, paid models.

1974

photographer
HANS FEURER

location
SEYCHELLES

month
MAY

'I like to make images that you can look at for a long period, that aren't
too definite; they can change meaning, give you new inspiration.'
(Hans Feurer)

1974

photographer
HANS FEURER

location
SEYCHELLES

month
JUNE

Here the natural quality of Feurer's approach is super-evident.
He achieves a touching intimacy with the model.

1974

photographer
HANS FEURER

location
SEYCHELLES

month
JULY

'I have a tendency to look for isolated places because I hate
to be disturbed…'
(Hans Feurer)

1974

photographer
HANS FEURER

location
SEYCHELLES

month
SEPTEMBER

Feurer's pictures catch the one exceptional split-second; they work at
the very limits of patience and technique. The girl submerged and leapt
and submerged and leapt again until an exposure of 1/1000th of a
second caught the water cascading from her.

1974

photographer
HANS FEURER

location
SEYCHELLES

month
OCTOBER

Making such pictures could be punishing. Feurer had Eva Nielsen
clean her teeth for half an hour. 'It is not too bad,' she said resignedly,
'my father was a dentist.'

1974

photographer
HANS FEURER

location
SEYCHELLES

month
NOVEMBER

Chichinou's sunglasses mirror the landscape at sunset.
A masterpiece of technique.

1974

photographer
HANS FEURER

location
SEYCHELLES

month
DECEMBER

Feurer's pictures made centre spreads and prime time television.
The Calendar seemed at its peak.

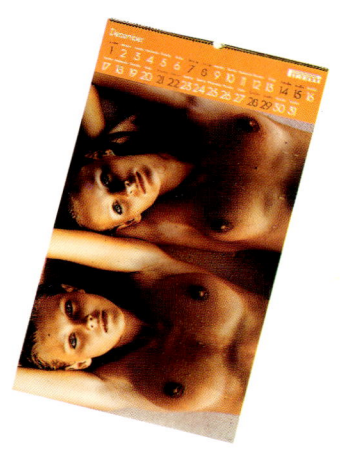

1 9 8 4

photographer
UWE OMMER

location
BAHAMAS

month
FEBRUARY

After a ten-year intermission the Calendar had to be reinvented. Was it remembered? Would it be noticed? It was decided once again to invoke sun, sea and sand in the Bahamas, but to introduce a new and specific marketing motif: the tread of the tyre.

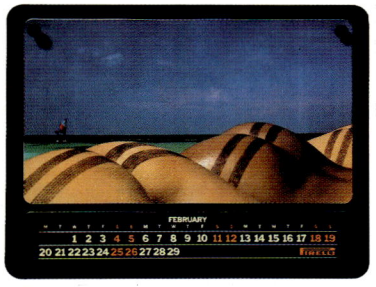

1984

photographer
UWE OMMER

location
BAHAMAS

month
APRIL

Martyn Walsh, art director, landed on Eleuthera bringing with him
neat, strong drawings and his props.

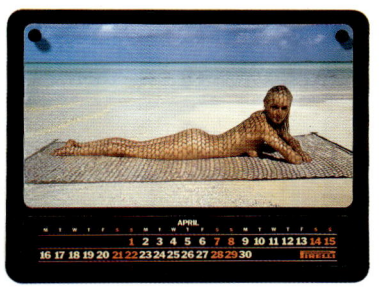

1984

photographer
UWE OMMER

location
BAHAMAS

month
OCTOBER

'We had an idea to sell, which is to show the tyre tread, and that makes
it different still from the other Calendars.'
(Uwe Ommer)

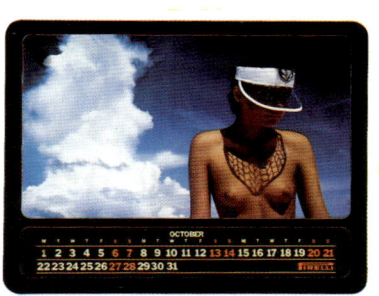

1984

photographer
UWE OMMER

location
BAHAMAS

month
DECEMBER

Ommer's eye for a graphic image – the old Pirelli tradition –
triumphed in the end.

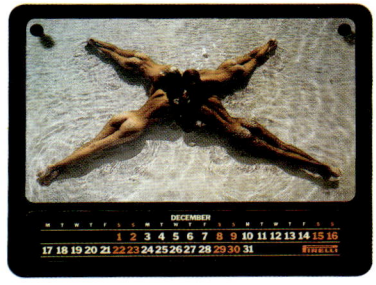

1985

photographer
NORMAN PARKINSON

location
EDINBURGH

month
JANUARY

This shoot found its inspiration in the fashion shows of Paris, and took place in Edinburgh's Assembly Rooms. 'Parks' was the doyen of fashion photographers, trained in days when you exposed only four sheets of film to fill three pages of a magazine.

1985

photographer
NORMAN PARKINSON

location
EDINBURGH

month
FEBRUARY

'My photographs – particularly my fashion photographs – are really a
portrait of the girl in the dress,' said Norman Parkinson, who saw
little difference, for the photographer, between *Vogue*
and the Pirelli Calendar.

1985

photographer
NORMAN PARKINSON

location
EDINBURGH

month
JUNE

'Whatever a situation we put a girl into, she really looks like she belongs… What's blatant is a turn-off.'
(Norman Parkinson)

1985

photographer
NORMAN PARKINSON

location
EDINBURGH

month
NOVEMBER

Martyn Walsh had conspired with twelve London fashion designers to
make a Pirelli collection of shoes, hats, frocks and capes, all
incorporating the tread. Here, the model is Iman.

1986

photographer
BERT STERN

location
THE COTSWOLDS

month
APRIL

Pirelli commissioned students at the Royal College of Art to paint
pictures that included the tyre tread and a naked woman. Bert Stern,
who had made the last pictures of Marilyn Monroe, photographed
the students' art and brought the model into the picture.

1986

photographer
BERT STERN

location
THE COTSWOLDS

month
NOVEMBER

'In America this would be very difficult to do, because the good models
wouldn't want to do pictures without their clothes on.'
(Bert Stern)

1 9 8 7

photographer
TERENCE DONOVAN

location
BATH

calendar
FRONT COVER

'Models can get something going in their head and hold it
until you capture it.'
(Donovan)

1987

photographer
TERENCE DONOVAN

location
BATH

month
MARCH

Martyn Walsh considered working in Brazil with maybe six black
models, the tyre tread shaped into the jewellery they wore.

1987

photographer
TERENCE DONOVAN

location
BATH

month
JUNE

A simple studio backdrop. 'I felt that the obsession with sand, sun and
sea had been saturated by previous Calendars. A simple, clean
approach seemed more appropriate.'
(Donovan)

1 9 8 7

photographer
TERENCE DONOVAN

location
BATH

month
JULY

'You have to create a sort of vacuum, and everyone is mustered in
the studio to get the job shot correctly; it is an
atmosphere of mental cleanliness.'
(Donovan)

1 9 8 7

photographer
TERENCE DONOVAN

location
BATH

month
AUGUST

The jewellery, inspired by that worn by the Kirdi women of Africa's
Mandara mountains, was made by Gerry Summers from designs
by Martyn Walsh.

1987

photographer
TERENCE DONOVAN

location
BATH

month
SEPTEMBER

'Everybody who is visually sophisticated accepts that black and white is much smarter than colour,' said Terence Donovan. It crossed his mind that a corporation would find it hard to go monochrome; it might look as if they could not afford colour. Yet the best black and white, printed to the highest standards, is quite as expensive. So Donovan kept the colours muted.

1988

photographer
BARRY LATEGAN

location
LONDON

month
JANUARY

As an art student, Martyn Walsh had met choreographer Gillian Lynne
long before she became renowned for shows like *Cats* and
Phantom of the Opera.

1988

photographer
BARRY LATEGAN

location
LONDON

month
MAY

The cast came from the principals of the Royal Ballet and from the chorus lines of shows and musicals. 'How well they danced took precedence over how good their bodies were.'
(Barry Lategan)

1 9 8 8

photographer
BARRY LATEGAN

location
LONDON

month
JUNE

Just improvising could never work. The brief was based on the seasons,
so Gillian Lynne made herself a scenario of the feelings
each month evoked.

1988

photographer
BARRY LATEGAN

location
LONDON

month
SEPTEMBER

The dancers' faces were disguised by metal masks fashioned by designer
Gerry Judah to resemble the fenders and fins of cars.

1988

photographer
BARRY LATEGAN

location
LONDON

month
OCTOBER

They worked in a movie studio in the Old Kent Road. The arabesque,
with its rise and fall of the dancers' bodies, came to symbolise the turn
of a wheel shod by Pirelli.

1989

photographer
JOYCE TENNESON

location
NEW YORK

month
DECEMBER-JANUARY

For this Calendar, Martyn Walsh chose the theme of astrology. This
first sheet represents Capricorn, the Goat, December 22 – January 20.
The kid's tread-stamped collar echoes the gold jewellery of 1987.

1 9 8 9

photographer
JOYCE TENNESON

location
NEW YORK

month
JANUARY-FEBRUARY

Moving into Aquarius. This Calendar maintained a consistent concept
and style throughout – a partnership between model and astrological
symbol, classical in its composition, and photographed in pale,
subtle tones.

1990

photographer
ARTHER ELGART

location
PUEBLA DEL RIO, SEVILLA

month
MARCH

Legend has it that from about 1,000 B.C. a religious festival was held
every four years at Olympia in honour of the goddess Hera. The
Herean games were an athletic contest in which only women competed.
In 706 B.C. the first men's athletics were staged at Olympia, which
thus became the birthplace of the Olympic Games.

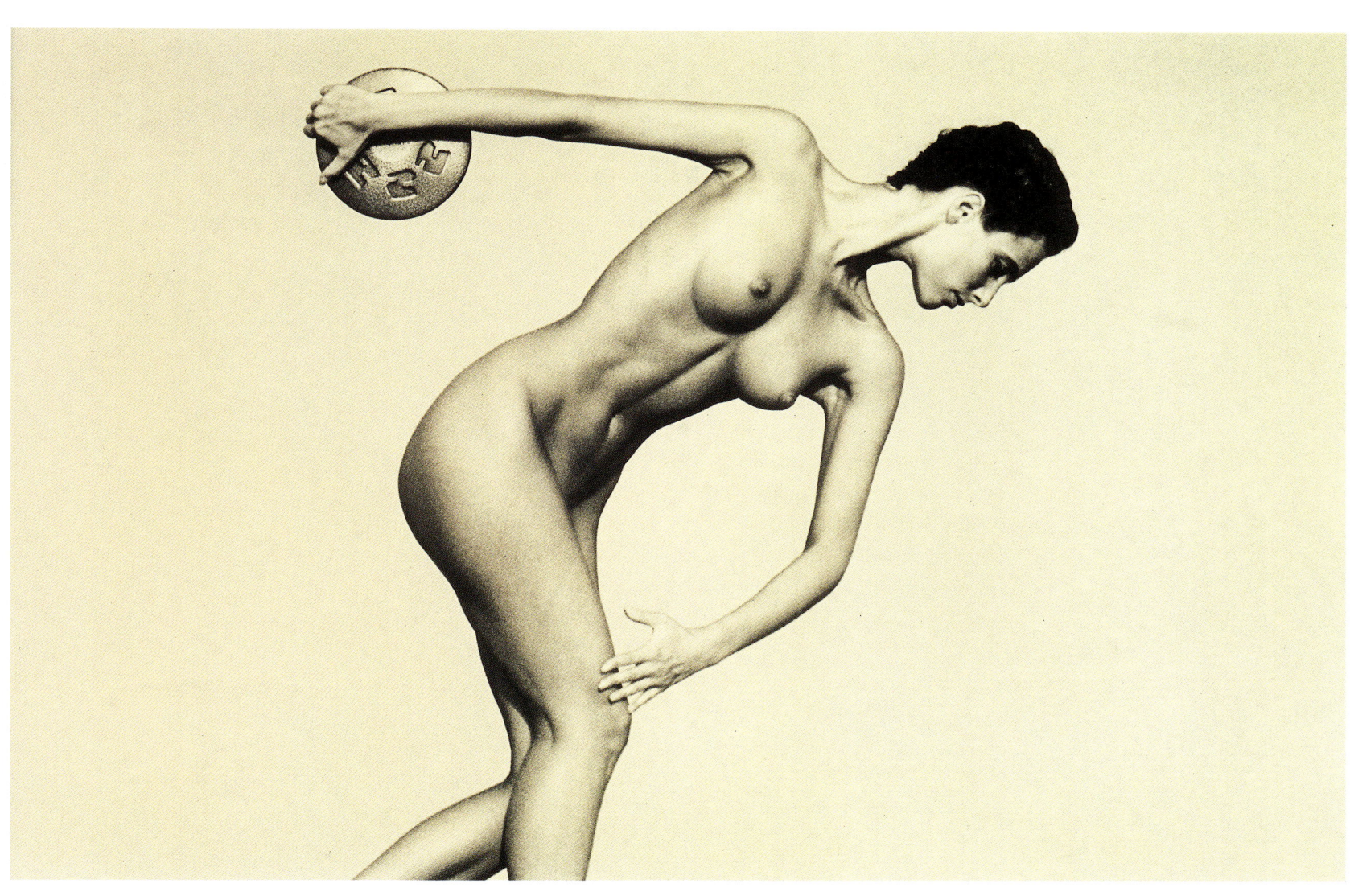

1990

photographer
ARTHER ELGART

location
PUEBLA DEL RIO, SEVILLA

month
JUNE

Martyn Walsh wished to pay tribute to Leni Riefenstahl, and in particular to her black and white documentary film of the 1936 Olympic Games in Berlin. This was the first and only Calendar to be shot in black and white. It was, as it is here, printed in four colours. Each picture represented different types of contest: throwing the discus, throwing the javelin, leaping hurdles, and passing the baton in relay.

1990

photographer
ARTHER ELGART

location
PUEBLA DEL RIO, SEVILLA

month
DECEMBER

The games are over and the winner, her brow garlanded with sprays of
olive, stands crowned according to the Herean rite.

1991

photographer
CLIVE ARROWSMITH

location
FRANCE

month
FEBRUARY

With what at the time seemed to be the dawn of a new era of peace in eastern Europe and beyond, Martyn Walsh wished to honour the role women have played in the defence of liberty. This Calendar featured heroines from history. Moscho Tzavella (1760-1803) defended the mountain village of Souli against Ali Pasha, the Turkish tyrant. Tzavella and the women of the village, armed only with sticks and stones, were victorious.

1991

photographer
CLIVE ARROWSMITH

location
FRANCE

month
MARCH

Anita Garibaldi (1819-1849) remains one of Brazil's foremost heroines.
Fighting alongside Giuseppe Garibaldi during the Civil War, she
earned the reputation of a fearless soldier. She and Guiseppe married in
1843 in Uraguay, where they fought unsuccessfully against Rosas, the
tyrannical Buenos Aires governor, at Rio Grande do Sul. On their
return to Italy, Anita and Giuseppe led a band of mercenaries to
victory in defence of Venice against the Austrians.

1991

photographer
CLIVE ARROWSMITH

location
FRANCE

month
JULY

Nzinga Mbande (1582-1653) fled the Portuguese invaders and created her own kingdom of Matamba. She led her refugee army through twenty years of war in a sustained effort to recover Ndongo, capital of Angola and once her brother's kingdom, until the invaders sued for peace. Queen Nzinga reconverted to Christianity and, diplomatic relations with Portugal having been restored, she ruled Matamba until her death at the age of eighty-one.

1992

photographer
CLIVE ARROWSMITH

location
ALMERIA

month
APRIL

Among many Chinese firsts is the calendar. According to the Chinese calendar, which is the oldest in the world, 1992 saw the year of the Monkey begin on 4 February. This Pirelli Calendar depicted the twelve animal signs of the Chinese horoscopes.
Here the Rabbit or Cat adopts a pose expressive of its typical finesse and trustworthiness. Among the Rabbits/Cats are Ingrid Bergman, Bob Hope and Queen Victoria.

1992

photographer
CLIVE ARROWSMITH

location
ALMERIA

month
JUNE

Here the Snake is poised in profound, intuitive concentration. Snakes seldom if ever make an important move without thinking long and hard. Greta Garbo, Mahatma Gandhi, J. F. Kennedy and Stirling Moss are among the Snakes.

1992

photographer
CLIVE ARROWSMITH

location
ALMERIA

month
SEPTEMBER

Legend tells of the Buddha naming the twelve years of the lunar cycle
after his twelve favourite animals. Here, the Monkey. Monkeys seldom
over-reach themselves and cope well with adversity. Leonardo da Vinci,
Charles Dickens, Omar Sharif, Elizabeth Taylor – all are Monkeys.

1993

photographer
JOHN CLARIDGE

location
SEYCHELLES

month
MARCH

To celebrate the thirtieth year since the first Pirelli Calendar, it was
decided to return to the original time-defying theme of beautiful girls
in an exotic setting.

1 9 9 3

photographer
JOHN CLARIDGE

location
SEYCHELLES

month
JUNE

Fashion designer Bruce Oldfield was commissioned to produce original
swimming costumes for this shoot. A fitting *envoi*…

1994

photographer
HERB RITTS

art director
DEREK FORSYTH

location
BAHAMAS

1994's Calendar will be Pirelli's twenty-first and takes us back to the
Bahamas. Here are photographer Herb Ritts and art director
Derek Forsyth on location, with models remaining discreetly
out of view until the launch.